The Little Book of
Oscar
WILDE

Catherine McIlvenna

Appletree

First published by Appletree Press Ltd
The Old Potato Station, 14 Howard Street South,
Belfast, BT7 1AP
Tel: +44 (0) 28 90 243074
Fax: +44 (0) 28 90 246756
E-mail: reception@appletree.ie
Web Site: www.irelandseye.com

Cover Illustrations © Corbis

The Little Book of Oscar Wilde

ISBN 0-86281-781-1

A record for this book is available from the British Library.

9 8 7 6 5 4 3 2 1

Contents

Introduction

' " I knew I should create a great sensation," gasped the Rocket and he went out.'

Born in Dublin on 16 October 1854, Oscar Wilde grew up in a wealthy and comfortable household. He was educated in Portora Royal, Enniskillen and Trinity College, Dublin, before embarking on a brilliant academic career at Oxford.

Married and settled in London, Wilde wrote short stories, fairy tales and the remarkable novel *The Picture of Dorian Gray*. His aestheticism and wit were self-proclaimed. His work as a playwright brought him public acclaim and success, most notably the sparkling comedy *The Importance of Being Earnest*.

He lived a flamboyant life, dazzling America on a lecture tour and English society with his vanity, self-promotion and talent. He created on stage the most shallow of society men and women, mocking the whims and morals of a self-conscious set. He conducted a debate on the merits of Art versus Realism. Generous, indulgent, passionate, he loved his friends heartily, entertaining them as only an Epicurean can. Wilde lived during an exciting and significant literary era. He kept company with Gide, Zola, Whistler, Shaw and Yeats. But the friendships were not always easy, as the bellicose, outspoken Wilde loved to tease and provoke the vanities of his friends.

His trial and subsequent imprisonment for "committing acts of gross indecency with other male persons" in 1895 ostracised Wilde and his family from Victorian respectability. Released from prison in 1897, Wilde went into exile; bankrupt, a pauper and a broken man. He died on 30 November 1900 in Paris. There are few people today who couldn't quote one of Oscar's lines. Whether it's an audacious boast, a coquettish aside or a poignant home truth, Oscar's wit is in common usage.

Collating this anthology, *The Little Book of Oscar Wilde*, is a treat any lover of literature would have enjoyed undertaking. But as with all pleasure, there is some pain. It is a personal and entirely subjective collection of Wilde's work. To revisit the four celebrated comedies and narrow the inclusion to short scenes from each play means some readers' favourite scenes have been left out. It has meant reading again the fables and daring to omit *The Selfish Giant* and choosing *The Happy Prince*. In my themed selection of quotations, I have tried to avoid those most oft repeated except when considering Lady Bracknell. How could anyone ignore her philosophy on the detriments of being discovered in a handbag? The selection of quotations is eclectic, juxtaposing the personal with the frivolous. It includes extracts from *De Profundis*, the frank and didactic letter Wilde wrote in prison to Alfred Douglas, and *The Decay of Lying* and both parts of *The Critic As Artist*, Wilde's dialectic on aestheticism. For further reading on Wilde's life and literary achievement, I include a short bibliography.

The Plays

Wilde wrote four comedies between 1892 and 1895: *Lady Windermere's Fan*; *A Woman of No Importance*; *An Ideal Husband*; and *The Importance of Being Earnest*.

These four plays are an holistic, scathing critique of aristocratic, Victorian society where reputations are easily ruined and non-conforming men and women outcast forever from respectable circles. Wilde chose his characters from the social elite and depicts a lifestyle of privilege, wealth, influence and affluence. Wilde locates his characters at prestigious London addresses which audiences would have associated with titled aristocrats, diplomats and ambassadors. On the surface, it appears to be a glittering, flighty world of dinner parties, afternoon tea and formal balls, but the lesser characters who gossip, judge and condemn indicate that this is a harsh world where any divergence from the social norm is swiftly chastised and the sinner ostracised.

In each play, one character has concealed a secret for years. In the case of Jack Worthing in *The Importance of Being Earnest*, an elaborate deceit has been created but is eventually revealed as truth. Mrs Arbuthnot in *A Woman of No Importance*, Mrs Erlynne in *Lady Windermere's Fan* and Lord Chiltern in *An Ideal Husband*, have each flouted social standards and their actions have grave implications. Wilde contrasts each sinner with a Puritan: Gerald, Mrs Arbuthnot's son; Mrs Erlynne's daughter, Lady Windermere; and Lord Chiltern's wife. These myopic characters adhere to staunch, unbending principles which are only relinquished after epiphanic experiences. With his characters accepting that imperfection is more human and tolerable, Wilde demonstrates the limitations of idealism.

In *Lady Windermere's Fan*, Mrs Erlynne who abandoned her baby daughter to run away with a lover twenty years earlier, returns and hopes to enter society again. She enlists the help of Lord Windermere, who is married to her daughter. He finances her sojourn in London and visits her frequently. Lord Windermere despises Mrs Erlynne, but anxious to prevent society discovering that Mrs Erlynne is his wife's mother and consequently rejecting Lady Windermere, he risks aspersions of adultery and arranges invitations to social events for Mrs Erlynne. It seems that Mrs Erlynne is threatening to expose her true identity to ensure Lord Windermere's help. Aware of rumours, jealous and angered by her husband's inexplicable friendship with Mrs Erlynne, Lady Windermere decides to accept Lord Darlington's love and leaves her husband and child. Lady Windermere is unaware that she is imitating her own mother's steps. Mrs Erlynne pursues her daughter to Lord Darlington's residence. The daughter harshly rejects her mother's advice to return to Lord Windermere. Supercilious and judgmental, initially she scorns Mrs Erlynne but is moved by plaintive advice and for the first time, mother comforts daughter. Before Lady Windermere has time to retreat and return home, Darlington arrives with Lord Windermere and Lord Augustus who had proposed marriage to Mrs Erlynne. To distract them and allow Lady Windermere to escape, Mrs Erlynne enters their company unannounced and unchaperoned. She exposes herself immediately to harsh criticism, her reputation is instantly blemished and she realises that Lord Augustus will withdraw his offer of marriage. Lady Windermere is touched by the stranger's selfless sacrifice and no longer tolerates any criticism of Mrs Erlynne. The play concludes with mother and daughter saying goodbye, Mrs Erlynne taking with her a photograph of her daughter and grandson. Mrs Erlynne is redeemed by saving her daughter from ruin, but to ensure that her daughter maintains her social status, Mrs Erlynne does not announce that she is her mother. Wilde illustrates how society exists on deception. At the end of the play, the daughter is still deceived and does not know who Mrs Erlynne is. Lord Windermere is deceived and will never know that his wife had left him for Lord Darlington.

A Woman of No Importance also treats the meeting of parent with a long lost child. In this play, it is an irresponsible father, Lord Illingworth, who is unintentionally reunited with his son, Gerald Arbuthnot. Lord Illingworth already knows and likes Gerald. He offers Gerald the opportunity to become his private secretary. Gerald is talented but poor and is flattered by the invitation to work for the Oxford-educated, wealthy aristocrat. Gerald is in love with Hester Worsley, an American millionairess. The position with Lord Illingworth will make Gerald eligible and able to court Hester. Set in a country house, women expound their acerbic epigrams on the irritation that is a faithful, loving husband. They are well aware of the restrictions and controls placed on women by society and hint that under the surface these codes are broken. Hester shows a disregard for the English class system and its restrictions. Lord Illingworth charms Mrs Allonby with his wit and levity but reveals a shallow nature, nonchalant to everyone. Mrs Arbuthnot arrives and recognises Lord Illingworth as the man who seduced her twenty years earlier. She loved and lived with him and gave birth to his son. He abandoned her and his son. When Gerald introduces his mother to his employer, he reunites his parents. Lord Illingworth immediately realises that Gerald is his son. Spiteful and suspicious of her former lover, Mrs Arbuthnot gives no reasons to Gerald for her objections to his becoming Illingworth's secretary. When she describes a scenario where a man seduces a young woman, Gerald's criticism is equally harsh on the foolish woman for allowing herself to be seduced. Mrs Arbuthnot withdraws her objection and Gerald is free to work for Lord Illingworth. Hester rejects Lord Illingworth's unwelcome attention. Enraged by this ill-treatment of Hester, Gerald instantly loses respect for Lord Illingworth and rejects the job offer. Gerald is only deterred from attacking Lord Illingworth when his mother reveals that he is Gerald's father. With a keen sense of moral duty and strictly adhering to a rigid moral code, Gerald attempts to persuade his mother to marry his father. His mother's emotional account of single parenthood enlightens and moves Hester. Gerald appreciates and recognises the worth of one reliable, unmarried parent's love. Hester and Gerald admit their love for each other. Hester, as a non-conformist, does not concern herself with Gerald's lack of social position or his illegitimate birth. When Lord Illingworth visits to claim his son, he is rejected by Mrs Arbuthnot. She also spurns his genuine marriage proposal which is more than twenty years too late. Mrs Arbuthnot has lived in shame until now, fear that Gerald will discover his origins and fear that he will suffer social humiliation because of his illegitimate origins. The ideal of marriage becomes unimportant and a life away from this society and its ideals beckons.

An Ideal Husband is a further exploration of human failure to conform to an ideal. Sir Robert Chiltern is the ideal husband; principled, upright, generous, loving, successful and already established as a brilliant politician with a great future predicted in the Cabinet. His wife worships and admires him, as long as he conforms to this defined ideal. The villain in this play is Mrs Cheveley who attends a party in the Chilterns' house. Lady Chiltern remembers her as a deceitful, treacherous and dishonest girl expelled from school. Mrs Cheveley has not come to redeem herself but demands Lord Chiltern's help. She expects his political support for a mining expedition which he has already judged to be a scam. Price and principles are themes in this play, with Mrs Cheveley certain she knows the virtuous Chiltern's price. In his youth, he sold a Cabinet secret to a foreign government and was rewarded with financial wealth. Mrs Cheveley has his original letter and is sure that the safe return of the letter in exchange for his support of the scam is the price of his principles. Chiltern agrees to her ultimatum but the intervention of Lady Chiltern makes him change his mind. Lady Chiltern is crushed by her husband's revelation, devastated by the idea that he is not honourable. Lord Goring, a close friend of the Chilterns and once engaged to Mrs Cheveley, retrieves the letter and spares his friend a scandal. Society is not offended because deception conceals the truth. Chiltern is offered a Cabinet post which he feels he must decline because his wife does not consider he deserves it. Once again, Lord Goring intervenes and Lady Chiltern finally realises that she must relinquish her narrow idealism. Much of the comedy lies in the secondary plot, where Lord Goring has been ordered to marry by his father, Lord Caversham. The father-son exchanges are tender and warm, contrasting with the austerity of Lady Chiltern and Mrs Cheveley.

The Importance of Being Earnest was first performed on 14 February 1895. Wilde subtitled the play A Trivial Comedy for Serious People. It is the wittiest, most light-hearted and least serious of all the comedies. The play begins with Jack Worthing returning to London from his stay in the country. He calls on his idle friend, Algy Moncrieff. They each admit to creating fictitious relations and using these relations to escape to or from the city. When he is bored in the country, Jack tells his ward, Cecily, that he must return to London to rescue his troublesome young brother Ernest. It is Jack who leads a double life; in London, he is Ernest and in the country he is Jack. Algy cites the deteriorating health of his friend Bunbury as an excuse to decline invitations to dine with relations. That afternoon, Algy is expecting a visit from his aunt Lady Bracknell and his cousin Gwendolen. In love with Gwendolen, Jack is determined to marry her. Jack's proposal to Gwendolen is hastily accepted. He has conformed to her lifelong ideal;

her desire to marry a man named Ernest. Lady Bracknell assesses Jack as a match for her daughter. He is judged unsuitable because he is an orphan and was discovered as a baby in a handbag at a London railway station. The censorious Lady Bracknell is quick to judge Jack and forbid his courtship of her daughter. Her defence is always by reference to society's expectations. Curious about Jack's other identity, Algy travels to the country and announces himself to Cecily as Jack's younger brother, Ernest. Cecily is already in love with him and engaged to him, the chief attraction being his name, Ernest.

Gwendolen arrives unannounced to visit her fiancé, Ernest. Cecily and Gwendolen are both engaged to Ernest, and bicker over who will be his wife. Both men are eager to be baptised and seek the help of Rev Chasuble. When the true names of Jack and Algy are identified, both men are rejected by their flighty fiancées who can only love a man named Ernest. Lady Bracknell is yet another unexpected visitor in the country and when she encounters and questions Cecily's tutor, Miss Prism, Jack's identity and roots are finally revealed. The elaborate deceit constructed and maintained by Jack is proven to be true. He is Algy's older brother and he was baptised Ernest more than twenty-eight years earlier. The comedy is propelled by farcical coincidences: the spontaneous arrival of Algy, Gwendolen, Jack and Lady Bracknell in the country and Lady Bracknell's recognition of Miss Prism who years earlier had lost the infant Jack. Jack is now elevated to his proper social status, his position is now entirely acceptable to Lady Bracknell and society.

The Importance of Being Earnest is considered Wilde's greatest play and *A Woman of No Importance* his weakest. It is a farcical comedy which always delights but it lacks the depth and complexity of *Lady Windermere's Fan*. *A Woman of No Importance* is admittedly melodramatic and in parts verbose but is astute in its analysis of female exploitation.

Shallow, good time Lord Goring is the most tolerant and magnanimous of all in *An Ideal Husband*. It is his gentle common sense which first alerts Lady Chiltern to her own unreasonable expectations and which succeeds in outwitting Mrs Cheveley.

In this anthology, two scenes have been selected from each comedy. From *Lady Windermere's Fan*, I have chosen the scene in Act 2 where Lord Darlington consoles Lady Windermere and declares his love for her. He offers her devotion forever, insouciant that coming away with him will cause a scandal. He challenges the hypocrisy of a society, which sacrifices happiness and love for respectability. Up until this time, Lady Windermere's outlook has been Puritanical but she does not easily resist his invitation. She wavers from her principles, but is held back by fear. The second scene presents the final meeting in Act Four between Mrs Erlynne, Lady Windermere and Lord Windermere. His contempt for Mrs Erlynne has been heightened because he saw her in Lord Darlington's residence. The daughter respects the stranger she had despised. Lady Windermere has experienced the stranger's generosity and she has recognised her own narrow-minded morality.

From *A Woman of No Importance*, both scenes involve dialogue between Lord Illingworth and Mrs Arbuthnot. The first, from Act 2, is the first meeting between the former lovers in over twenty years. Lord Illingworth is anxious that Gerald is allowed to accept the post as private secretary. Initially, Mrs Arbuthnot's captious objection seems to be to spite Lord Illingworth. As she emotionally recounts the past, her real objection is a fear of losing her son. The second scene is taken from Act 4. Lord Illingworth visits Mrs Arbuthnot, to request full-time fatherhood to Gerald. Mrs Arbuthnot banishes Illingworth from both their lives. His position is one of quiet desperation, which he conceals with casual scorn.

He pledges his inheritance to Gerald and proposes marriage to Mrs Arbuthnot, but there is no reciprocation. Unable to restore a relationship with either his son or his former lover, Lord Illingworth leaves.

In *An Ideal Husband*, the first scene selected is a conversation in Act 2 between Lady Chiltern and Lord Goring. Already aware of Lord Chiltern's guilty secret, Lord Goring subtly indicates that setting an ideal as a standard is unreasonable. Lady Chiltern clings truculently to her idealistic belief in the perfection of Lord Chiltern. The light-hearted exchanges between Mabel Chiltern and Lord Goring keep the secondary subplot ticking over. The second scene is taken from the end of Act 2, where Mrs Cheveley calls on Lady Chiltern. The loathing is mutual between them. Mrs Cheveley delights in mocking Lady Chiltern's morality and announces that Lord Chiltern's wealth was earned by dishonourable behaviour. Alone with his wife, Lord Chiltern admits his past. Repelled by the knowledge that her husband is flawed, Lady Chiltern rejects him. Lord Chiltern exposes her mistake in creating and loving such an ideal. His is a plea for mature and unconditional love.

From *The Importance of Being Earnest*, I have chosen the scene in Act 2 which is the first meeting between Cecily and Gwendolen. The women observe superficial social etiquette, Gwendolen from the town assuming superiority over the younger, country Cecily. The shallow friendship quickly and humorously deteriorates as each regards the other as an interloper in Ernest's affections. They are reunited only when they discover that there is no Ernest and that both engagements are sham. The final scene in Act 3 has also been selected, where Jack's identity is at last revealed. All ends well, even for Miss Prism, who has her invaluable handbag restored and has found an admirer.

Lady Windermere's Fan – From Act 2

[*They pass into the ball-room, and Lady Windermere and Lord Darlington enter from the terrace.*]

LADY WINDEREMERE.   Yes. Her coming here is monstrous, unbearable. I know now what you meant today at tea time. Why didn't you tell me right out? You should have!

LORD DARLINGTON.   I couldn't! A man can't tell these things about another man! But if I had known he was going to make you ask her here tonight, I think I would have told you. That insult, at any rate, you would have been spared.

LADY WINDERMERE.   I did not ask her. He insisted on her coming – against my entreaties – against my commands. Oh! the house is tainted for me! I feel that every woman here sneers at me as she dances by with my husband. What have I done to deserve this? I gave him all my life. He took it – used it – spoiled it! I am degraded in my own eyes; and I lack courage – I am a coward! [*Sits down on sofa.*]

LORD DARLINGTON.   If I know you at all, I know that you can't live with a man who treats you like this! What sort of life would you have with him? You would feel that he was lying to you every moment of the day. You would feel that the look in his eyes was false, his voice false, his touch false, his passion false. He would come to you when he was weary of others; you would have to charm him. You would have to be to him the mask of his real life, the cloak to hide his secret.

LADY WINDEREMERE.   You are right – you are terribly right . But where am I to turn? You said you would be my friend, Lord Darlington. – Tell me, what am I to do? Be my friend now.

LORD DARLINGTON.   Between men and women there is no friendship possible. There is passion, enmity, worship, love, but no friendship. I love you –

LADY WINDERMERE.   No, no! *[Rises.]*

LORD DARLINGTON.   Yes, I love you! You are more to me than anything in the whole world. What does your husband give you? Nothing. Whatever is in him he gives to this wretched woman, whom he has thrust into your society, into your home, to shame you before every one. I offer you my life –

LADY WINDERMERE.   Lord Darlington!

LORD DARLINGTON.   My life – my whole life. Take it, and do with it what you will .... I love you – love you as I have never loved any thing living. From the moment I met you I loved you, loved you blindly, adoringly, madly! You did not know it then – you know it now! Leave this tonight. I won't tell you that the world matters nothing, or the world's voice, or the voice of society. They matter a great deal. They matter far too much. But there are moments when one has to choose between living one's own life, fully, entirely, completely – or dragging out some false, shallow, degrading existence that the world in its hypocrisy demands. You have that moment now. Choose! Oh, my love, choose!

LADY WINDERMERE *[Moving slowly away from him, and looking at him with startled eyes.]* I have not the courage.

LORD DARLINGTON *[Following her.]* Yes, you have the courage. There may be six months of pain, of disgrace even, but when you no longer bear his name, when you bear mine, all will be well. Margaret, my love, my wife that shall be some day – yes, my wife! You know it! What are you now? This woman has the place that belongs by right to you. Oh! go – go out of this house, with head erect, with a smile upon your lips, with courage in your eyes. All London will know why you did it; and who will blame you? No one. If they do, what matter? Wrong? What is wrong? It's wrong for a man to abandon his wife for a shameless woman. It is wrong for a wife to remain with a man who so dishonours her. You said once you would make no compromise with things. Make none now. Be brave! Be yourself!

LADY WINDERMERE.   I am afraid of being myself. Let me think! Let me wait! My husband may return to me. [Sits down on sofa.]

LORD DARLINGTON.   And you would take him back! You are not what I thought you were. You are just the same as every other woman. You would stand anything rather than face the censure of a world, whose praise you would despise.   In a week you will be driving with this woman in the Park. She will be your constant guest – your dearest friend. You would endure anything rather than break with one blow this monstrous tie. You are right. You have no courage; none!

LADY WINDERMERE.   Ah, give me time to think. I cannot answer you now.

[Passes her hand nervously over her brow.]

LORD DARLINGTON.   It must be now or not at all.

LADY WINDERMERE [Rising from the sofa.]   Then, not at all!

[A pause.]

LORD DARLINGTON.   You break my heart!

LADY WINDERMERE.   Mine is already broken.

[A pause.]

LORD DARLINGTON.   Tomorrow I leave England. This is the last time I shall ever look on you. You will never see me again. For one moment our lives met – our souls touched. They must never meet or touch again. Goodbye, Margaret.

[Exit.]

Lady Windermere's Fan – From Act 4

MRS ERLYNNE [With a note of irony in her voice.] To bid goodbye to my dear daughter, of course. [Lord Windermere bites his under lip in anger. Mrs Erlynne looks at him, and her voice and manner become serious. In her accents as she talks there is a note of deep tragedy. For a moment she reveals herself.] Oh, don't imagine I am going to have a pathetic scene with her, weep on her neck and tell her who I am, and all that kind of thing. I have no ambition to play the part of a mother. Only once in my life have I know a mother's feelings. That was last night. They were terrible – they made me suffer – they made me suffer too much. For twenty years, as you say, I have lived childless – I want to live childless still. [Hiding her feelings with a trivial laugh.] Besides, my dear Windermere, how on earth could I pose as a mother with a grown-up daughter? Margaret is twenty-one, and I have never admitted that I am more than twenty-nine or thirty at the most. Twenty-nine when there are pink shades, thirty when there are not. So you see what difficulties it would involve. No, as far as I am concerned, let your wife cherish the memory of this dead, stainless mother. Why should I interfere with her illusions? I find it hard enough to keep my own. I lost one illusion last night, I thought I had no heart. I find I have, and a heart doesn't suit me, Windermere. Somehow it doesn't go with modern dress. It makes one look old. *[Takes up hand-mirror from table and looks into it.]* And it spoils one's career at critical moments.

LORD WINDERMERE.   You fill me with horror – with absolute horror.

MRS ERLYNNE *[Rising.]*   I suppose, Windermere, you would like me to retire into a convent or become a hospital nurse, or something of that kind, as people do in silly modern novels. That is stupid of you, Arthur; in real life we don't do such things – not as long as we have any good looks left, at any rate. No – what consoles one nowadays is not repentance, but pleasure. Repentance is quite out of date. And besides, if a woman really repents, she has to go to a bad dressmaker, otherwise no one believes in her. And nothing in the world would induce me to do that. No; I am going to pass entirely out of your two lives. My coming into them has been a mistake – I discovered that last night.

LORD WINDERMERE.   A fatal mistake.

MRS ERLYNNE *[Smiling.]*   Almost fatal.

LORD WINDERMERE.   I am sorry now I did not tell my wife the whole thing at once.

MRS ERLYNNE.   I regret my bad actions. You regret your good ones – that is the difference between us.

LORD WINDERMERE.   I don't trust you. I will tell my wife. It's better for her to know, and from me. It will cause her infinite pain – it will humiliate her terribly, but it's right that she should know.

MRS ERLYNNE.   You propose to tell her?

LORD WINDERMERE.   I am going to tell her.

MRS ERLYNNE [Going up to him.]   If you do, I will make my name so infamous that it will mar every moment of her life. It will ruin her, and make her wretched. If you dare to tell her, there is no depth of degradation I will not sink to, no pit of shame I will not enter. You shall not tell her – I forbid you.
LORD WINDERMERE.   Why?

MRS ERLYNNE [After a pause.]   If I said to you that I cared for her, perhaps loved her even – you would sneer at me, wouldn't you?

LORD WINDERMERE.   I should feel it was not true. A mother's love means devotion, unselfishness, sacrifice. What could you know of such things?

MRS ERLYNNE. You are right. What could I know of such things? Don't let us talk any more about it – as for telling my daughter who I am, that I do not allow. It is my secret, it is not yours. If I make up my mind to tell her, and I think I will, I shall tell her before I leave the house – if not, I shall never tell her.

LORD WINDERMERE [Angrily.)   Then let me beg of you to leave our house at once. I will make your excuses to Margaret.
[Enter Lady Windermere R. She goes over to Mrs Erlynne with the photograph in her hand. Lord Windermere moves to back of sofa, and anxiously watches Mrs Erlynne as the scene progresses.]

LADY WINDERMERE.   I am so sorry, Mrs Erlynne, to have kept you waiting. I couldn't find the photograph anywhere. At last I discovered it in my husband's dressing-room – he had stolen it.

MRS ERLYNNE [*Takes the photograph from her and looks at it.*] I am not surprised – it is charming.[*Goes over to sofa with Lady Windermere, and sits down beside her. Looks again at the photograph.*] And so that is your little boy! What is he called?

LADY WINDERMERE.   Gerard, after my dear father.

MRS ERLYNNE [*Laying the photograph down.*]   Really?

LADY WINDERMERE.   Yes. If it had been a girl, I would have called it after my mother. My mother had the same name as myself, Margaret.

MRS EYLYNNE.   My name is Margaret too.

LADY WINDERMERE.   Indeed!

MRS ERLYNNE.   Yes. [*Pause.*] You are devoted to your mother's memory, Lady Windermere, your husband tells me.

LADY WINDERMERE.   We all have ideals in life. At least we all should have. Mine is my mother.

MRS ERLYNNE.   Ideals are dangerous things. Realities are better. They wound, but they're better.

LADY WINDERMERE [*Shaking her head.*]   If I lost my ideals, I should lose everything.

MRS ERLYNNE.   Everything?

LADY WINDERMERE.   Yes. [*Pause.*]

MRS ERLYNNE.   Did you father often speak to you of your mother?

LADY WINDERMERE.   No, it gave him too much pain. He told me how my mother had died a few months after I was born. His eyes had filled with tears as he spoke. Then he begged me never to mention her name to him again. It made him suffer even to hear it. My father – my father really died of a broken heart. His was the most ruined life I know.

MRS ERLYNNE *[Rising.]*   I am afraid I must go now, Lady Windermere.

LADY WINDERMERE *[Rising.)*   Oh no, don't.

MRS ERLYNNE.   I think I had better. My carriage must have come back by this time. I sent it to Lady Jedburgh's with a note.

LADY WINDERMERE.   Arthur, would you mind seeing if Mrs Erlynne's carriage has come back?

MRS ERLYNNE.   Pray don't trouble, Lord Windermere.

LADY WINDERMERE.   Yes, Arthur, do go, please.

[Lord Windermere hesitates for a moment and looks at Mrs Erlynne. She remains quite impassive. He leaves the room.]

[To Mrs Erlynne.]   Oh! What am I to say to you? You saved me last night.

[Goes towards her.]

MRS ERLYNNE. Hush – don't speak of it.

LADY WINDERMERE.   I must speak of it. I can't let you think that I am going to accept this sacrifice. I am not. It is too great. I am going to tell my husband everything. It is my duty.

MRS ERLYNNE.   It is not your duty – at least you have duties to others besides him. You say you owe me something?

LADY WINDERMERE.   I owe you everything.

MRS ERLYNNE.   Then pay your debt by silence. That is the only way in which it can be paid. Don't spoil the one good thing I have done in my life by telling it to any one. Promise me that what passed last night will remain a secret between us. You must not bring misery into your husband's life. Why spoil his love? You must not spoil it. Love is easily killed. Oh! how easily love is killed! Pledge me your word, Lady Windermere, that you will never tell him. I insist upon it.

LADY WINDERMERE *[With bowed head.]*   It is your will, not mine.

MRS ERLYNNE.   Yes, it is my will. And never forget your child – I like to think of you as a mother. I like to think of yourself as one.

LADY WINDERMERE *[Looking up.]*   I always will now. Only once in my life I have forgotten my own mother – that was last night. Oh, if I had remembered her I should not have been so foolish, so wicked.

MRS ERLYNNE *[With a slight shudder.]*   Hush, last night is quite over.

[Enter Lord Windermere.]

LORD WINDERMERE.   Your carriage has not come back yet, Mrs Erlynne.

MRS ERLYNNE. It makes no matter. I'll take a hansom. There is nothing in the world so respectable as a good

Shrewsbury and Talbot. And now, dear Lady Windermere, I am afraid it is really goodbye. *[Moves up C.]* Oh, I remember. You'll think me absurd, but do you know I've taken a great fancy to this fan that I was silly enough to run away with last night from your ball. Now, I wonder would you give it to me? Lord Windermere says you may. I know it is his present.

LADY WINDERMERE.   Oh, certainly, if it will give you any pleasure. But it has my name on it. It has 'Margaret' on it.

MRS ERLYNNE.   But we have the same Christian name.

LADY WINDERMERE.   Oh, I forgot. Of course, do have it. What a wonderful chance our names being the same!

MRS ERLYNNE.   Quite wonderful. Thanks – it will always remind me of you. *[Shakes hands with her.]*

[Enter Parker.]

PARKER.   Lord Augustus Lorton. Mrs Erlynne's carriage has come.

[Enter Lord Augustus.]

LORD AUGUSTUS.   Good morning, dear boy. Good morning, Lady Windermere. *[Sees Mrs Erlynne.]* Mrs Erlynne!

MRS ERLYNNE.   How do you do, Lord Augustus? Are you quite well this morning?

LORD AUGUSTUS *[Coldly.]*   Quite well, thank you, Mrs Erlynne.

MRS ERLYNNE. You don't look at all well, Lord Augustus. You stop up too late – it is so bad for you. You really should take more care of yourself. Goodbye, Lord Windermere. [*Goes towards door with a bow to Lord Augustus. Suddenly smiles and looks back at him.*] Lord Augustus! Won't you see me to my carriage? You might carry the fan.

LORD WINDERMERE. Allow me!

MRS ERLYNNE. No; I want Lord Augustus. I have a special message for the dear Duchess. Won't you carry the fan, Lord Augustus?

LORD AUGUSTUS. If you really desire it, Mrs Erlynne.

MRS ERLYNNE [*Laughing.*] Of course I do. You'll carry it so gracefully. You would carry off anything gracefully, dear Lord Augustus.

[*When she reaches the door she looks back for a moment at Lady Windermere. Their eyes meet. Then she turns, and exit C. followed by Lord Augustus.*]

LADY WINDERMERE. You will never speak against Mrs Erlynne again, Arthur, will you?

LORD WINDERMERE [*Gravely.*] She is better than one thought her.

LADY WINDERMERE. She is better than I am.

LORD WINDERMERE [*Smiling as he strokes her hair.*] Child, you and she belong to different worlds. Into your world evil has never entered.

LADY WINDERMERE. Don't say that, Arthur. There is the same world for all of us, and good and evil, sin and innocence, go through it hand in hand. To shut one's eyes to half of life that one may live securely is as though one blinded oneself that one might walk with more safety in a land of pit and precipice.

LORD WINDERMERE *[Moves down with her.]* Darling, why do you say that?

LADY WINDERMERE *[Sits on sofa.]* Because I, who had shut my eyes to life, came to the brink. And one who had separated us –

LORD WINDERMERE. We were never separated.

LADY WINDERMERE. We never must be again. Oh Arthur, don't love me less, and I will trust you more. I will trust you absolutely. Let us go to Selby. In the Rose Garden at Selby the roses are white and red.

[Enter Lord Augustus C.]

LORD AUGUSTUS. Arthur, she has explained everything!

[Lady Windermere looks horribly frightened at this. Lord Windermere starts. Lord Augustus takes Windermere by the arm and brings him to front of stage. He talks rapidly and in a low voice. Lady Windermere stands watching them in terror.]

My dear fellow, she has explained every demmed thing. We all wronged her immensely. It was entirely for my sake she went to Darlington's rooms. Called first at the Club – fact is, wanted to put me out of suspense – and being told I had gone on – followed – naturally frightened when she heard a lot of us coming in – retired to another room – I assure you, most gratifying to me, the whole thing. We all behaved brutally to her. She is just the woman for me. Suits me down to the ground. All the conditions she makes are that we live entirely out of England. A very good thing, too. Demmed clubs, demmed climate, demmed cooks, demmed everything. Sick of it all!

LADY WINDERMERE. *[Frightened.]* Has Mrs Erlynne –?

LORD AUGUSTUS. *[Advancing towards her with a low bow.]* Yes, Lady Windermere – Mrs Erlynne has done me the honour of accepting my hand.

LORD WINDERMERE. Well, you are certainly marrying a very clever woman!

LADY WINDERMERE. *[Taking her husband's hand.]* Ah, you're marrying a very good woman!

CURTAIN

A Woman Of No Importance – From Act 2

GERALD. Mother, this is Lord Illingworth, who has offered to take me as his private secretary.

MRS ARBUTHNOT *(bows coldly.)*

It is a wonderful opening for me, isn't it? I hope he won't be disappointed in me, that is all. You'll thank Lord Illingworth, mother, won't you?

MRS ARBUTHNOT. Lord Illingworth is very good, I am sure, to interest himself in you for the moment.

LORD ILLINGWORTH *[putting his hand on Gerald's shoulder.]* Oh, Gerald and I are great friends already Mrs...Arbuthnot.

MRS ARBUTHNOT. There can be nothing in common between you and my son, Lord Illingworth.

GERALD.   Dear mother, how can you say so? Of course, Lord Illingworth is awfully clever and that sort of thing. There is nothing Lord Illingworth doesn't know.

LORD ILLINGWORTH.   My dear boy!

GERALD.   He knows more about life than any one I have ever met. I feel an awful duffer when I am with you, Lord Illingworth. Of course, I have had so few advantages. I have not been to Eton or Oxford like other chaps. But Lord Illingworth doesn't seem to mind that. He has been awfully good to me, mother.

MRS ARBUTHNOT.   Lord Illingworth may change his mind. He may not really want you as his secretary.

GERALD.   Mother!

MRS ARBUTHNOT.   You must remember, as you said yourself, you have had so few advantages.

MRS ALLONBY.   Lord Illingworth, I want to speak to you for a moment. Do come over.

LORD ILLINGWORTH.   Will you excuse me, Mrs Arbuthnot? Now, don't let your charming mother make any more difficulties, Gerald. The thing is quite settled, isn't it?

GERALD.   I hope so.

(Lord Illingworth goes across to Mrs Allonby.)

MRS ALLONBY.   I thought you were never going to leave the lady in black velvet.

LORD ILLINGWORTH.   She is excessively handsome. [Looks at Mrs Arbuthnot.]

LADY HUNSTANTON.   Caroline, shall we all make a move to the music-room? Miss Worsley is going to play. You'll come too, dear Mrs Arbuthnot, won't you? You don't know what a treat is in store for you. *[To Doctor Daubeny.]* I must really take Miss Worsley down some afternoon to the rectory. I should so much like dear Mrs Daubeny to hear her on the violin. Ah, I forgot. Dear Mrs Daubeny's hearing is a little defective, is it not?

THE ARCHDEACON.   Her deafness is a great privation to her. She can't even hear my sermons now. She reads them at home. But she has many resources in herself, many resources.

LADY HUNSTANTON.   She reads a good deal, I suppose?

THE ARCHDEACON.   Just the very largest print. The eyesight is rapidly going. But she's never morbid, never morbid.

GERALD *[to Lord Illingworth.]*   Do speak to my mother, Lord Illingworth, before you go into the music-room. She seems to think, somehow, you don't mean what you said to me.

MRS ALLONBY.   Aren't you coming?

LORD ILLINGWORTH.   In a few moments. Lady Hunstanton, if Mrs. Arbuthnot would allow me, I would like to say a few words to her, and we will join you later on.

LADY HUNSTANTON.   Ah, of course. You will have a great deal to say to her, and she will have a great deal to thank you for. It is not every son who gets such an offer, Mrs. Arbuthnot. But I know you will appreciate that, dear!

LADY CAROLINE.   John!

LADY HUNSTANTON.   Now, don't keep Mrs. Arbuthnot too long, Lord Illingworth. We can't spare her.

[*Exit following the other guests. Sound of violin heard from music-room.*]

LORD ILLINGWORTH.   So that is our son, Rachel! Well, I am very proud of him. He is a Hartford, every inch of him. By the way, why Arbuthnot, Rachel?

MRS ARBUTHNOT.   One name is as good as another, when one has no right to any name.

LORD ILLINGWORTH.   I suppose so – but why Gerald?

MRS ARBUTHNOT.   After a man whose heart I broke – after my father.

LORD ILLINGWORTH.   Well, Rachel, what is over is over. All I have got to say now is that I am very, very much pleased with our boy. The world will know him merely as my private secretary, but to me he will be something very near, and very dear. It is a curious thing, Rachel, that my life seemed to be quite complete. It was not so. It lacked something, it lacked a son. I have found my son now. I am glad I have found him.

MRS ARBUTHNOT.   You have no right to claim him, or the smallest part of him. The boy is entirely mine, and shall remain mine.

LORD ILLINGWORTH.   My dear Rachel, you have had him to yourself for over twenty years. Why not let me have him for a little now? He is quite as much mine as yours.

MRS ARBUTHNOT.   Are you talking of the child you abandoned? Of the child who, as far as you are concerned, might have died of hunger and of want?

LORD ILLINGWORTH.   You forget, Rachel, it was you who left me. It was not I who left you.

MRS ARBUTHNOT.   I left you because you refused to give the child a name. Before my son was born, I implored you to marry me.

LORD ILLINGWORTH.   I had no expectations then. And besides, Rachel, I wasn't much older than you were. I was only twenty-two. I was only twenty-one, I believe, when the whole thing began in your father's garden.

MRS ARBUTHNOT.   When a man is old enough to do wrong he should be old enough to do right also.

LORD ILLINGWORTH.   My dear Rachel, intellectual generalities are always interesting, but generalities in morals mean nothing. As for saying I left our child to starve, that, of course, is untrue and silly. My mother offered you six hundred a year. But you wouldn't take anything. You simply disappeared, and carried the child away with you.

MRS. ARBUTHNOT.   I wouldn't have accepted a penny from her. Your father was different. He told you, in my presence, when we were in Paris, that it was your duty to marry me.

LORD ILLINGWORTH.   Oh, duty is what one expects from others, it is not what one does oneself. Of course, I was influenced by my mother. Every man is when he is young.

MRS ARBUTHNOT.   I am glad to hear you say so. Gerald shall certainly not go away with you.

LORD ILLINGWORTH.   What nonsense, Rachel!

MRS ARBUTHNOT.   Do you think I would allow my son –

LORD ILLINGWORTH.   Our son.

MRS ARBUTHNOT.   My son – *[Lord Illingworth shrugs his shoulders.]* – to go away with the man who spoiled my youth, ruined my life, who has tainted every moment of my days? You don't realise what my past has been in suffering and shame.

LORD ILLINGWORTH.   My dear Rachel, I must candidly say that I think Gerald's future considerably more important than your past.

MRS ARBUTHNOT.   Gerald cannot separate his future from my past.

LORD ILLINGWORTH.   That is exactly what he should do. That is exactly what you should help him to do. What a typical woman you are! You talk sentimentally and you are thoroughly selfish the whole time. But don't let us have a scene. Rachel, I want you to look at this matter from the common-sense point of view, from the point of view of what is best for our son, leaving you and me out of the question. What is our son at present? An underpaid clerk in a small Provincial Bank in a third-rate English town. If you imagine he is quite happy in such a position, you are mistaken. He is thoroughly discontented.

MRS ARBUTHNOT.   He was not discontented till he met you. You have made him so.

LORD ILLINGWORTH.   Of course I made him so. Discontent is the first step in the progress of a man or a nation. But I did not leave him with a mere longing for things he could not get. No, I made him a charming offer. He jumped at it, I need hardly say. Any young man would. And now, simply because it turns out that I am the boy's own father and he my own son, you propose practically to ruin his career. That is to say, if I were a stranger, you would allow Gerald to go away with me, but as he is my own flesh and blood you won't. How utterly illogical you are!

MRS ARBUTHNOT.   I will not allow him to go.

LORD ILLINGWORTH.   How can you prevent it? What excuse can you give him for making him decline such an offer as mine? I won't tell him in what relations I stand to him, I need hardly say. But you daren't tell him. You know that. Look how you have brought him up.

MRS ARBUTHNOT.   I have brought him up to be a good man.

LORD ILLINGWORTH.   Quite so. And what is the result? You have educated him to be your judge if he ever finds you out. And a bitter, an unjust judge he will be to you. Don't be deceived, Rachel. Children begin by loving their parents. After a time they judge them. Rarely, if ever, do they forgive them.

MRS ARBUTHNOT.   George, don't take my son away from me. I have had twenty years of sorrow, and I have only had one thing to love me, only one thing to love. You have had a life of joy, and pleasure, and success. You have been quite happy, you have never thought of us. There was no reason, according to your views of life, why you should have remembered us at all. Your meeting us was a mere accident, a horrible accident. Forget it. Don't come now, and rob me of – of all I have in the whole world. You are so rich in other things. Leave me the little vineyard of my life; leave me the walled-in garden and the well of water; the ewe-lamb Gód sent me, in pity or in wrath, oh! leave me that. George, don't take Gerald from me.

LORD ILLINGWORTH.   Rachel, at the present moment you are not necessary to George's career; I am. There is nothing more to be said on the subject.

MRS ARBUTHNOT.   I will not let him go.

LORD ILLINGWORTH.   Here is Gerald. He has a right to decide for himself.

A Woman Of No Importance – From Act 4

MRS ARBUTHNOT.   You come too late. My son has no need of you. You are not necessary.

LORD ILLINGWORTH.   What do you mean, Rachel?

MRS ARBUTHNOT.   That you are not necessary to Gerald's career. He does not require you.

LORD ILLINGWORTH.   I do not understand you.

MRS ARBUTHNOT.   Look into the garden. *[Lord Illingworth rises and looks towards the window.]* You had better not let them see you; you bring unpleasant memories. *[Lord Illingworth looks out and starts.]* She loves him. They love each other. We are safe from you, and we are going away.

LORD ILLINGWORTH.   Where?

MRS. ARBUTHNOT.   We will not tell you, and if you find us we will not know you. You seem surprised. What welcome would you get from the girl whose lips you tried to soil, from the boy whose life you have shamed, from the mother whose dishonour comes from you?

LORD ILLINGWORTH.   You have grown hard, Rachel.

MRS ARBUTHNOT.   I was too weak once. It is well for me that I have changed.

LORD ILLINGWORTH.   I was very young at the time. We men know life too early.

MRS ARBUTHNOT.   And we women know life too late. That is the difference between men and women. *[A pause.]*

LORD ILLINGWORTH.   Rachel, I want my son. My money may be of no use to him now. I may be of no use to him, but I want my son. Bring us together, Rachel. You can do it if you choose. *[Sees letter on table.]*

MRS ARBUTHNOT.   There's no room in my boy's life for you. He is not interested in you.

LORD ILLINGWORTH.   Then why does he write to me?

MRS ARBUTHNOT.   What do you mean?

LORD ILLINGWORTH.   What letter is this?
[Takes up letter.]

MRS. ARBUTHNOT.   That – is nothing. Give it to me.

LORD ILLINGWORTH.   It is addressed to me.

MRS ARBUTHNOT.   You are not to open it. I forbid you to open it.

LORD ILLINGWORTH.   And in Gerald's handwriting.

MRS ARBUTHNOT.   It was not to have been sent. It is a letter he wrote to you this morning, before he saw me. But he is sorry now he wrote it, very sorry. You are not to open it. Give it to me.

LORD ILLINGWORTH.   It belongs to me. *[Opens it, sits down and reads it slowly. Mrs. Arbuthnot watches him all the time.]* You have read this letter, I suppose, Rachel?

MRS ARBUTHNOT.   No.

LORD ILLINGWORTH.   You know what is in it?

MRS ARBUTHNOT.   Yes!

LORD ILLINGWORTH.   I don't admit for a moment
that the boy is right in what he says. I don't admit that it
is any duty of mine to marry you. I deny it entirely. But to
get my son back I am ready – yes, I am ready to marry
you, Rachel – and to treat you always with the deference
and respect due to my wife. I will marry you as soon as
you choose. I give you my word of honour.

MRS ARBUTHNOT.   You made that promise to me once
before and broke it.

LORD ILLINGWORTH.   I will keep it now. And that
will show you that I love my son, at least as much as you
love him. For when I marry you, Rachel, there are some
ambitions I shall have to surrender. High ambitions, too, if
any ambition is high.

MRS ARBUTHNOT.   I decline to marry you, Lord
Illingworth.

LORD ILLINGWORTH.   Do tell me your reasons. They
would interest me enormously.

MRS ARBUTHNOT.   I have already explained them to
my son.

LORD ILLINGWORTH.   I suppose they were intensely
sentimental, weren't they? You women live by your
emotions and for them. You have no philosophy of life.

MRS ARBUTHNOT.   You are right. We women live by
our emotions and for them. By our passions, and for them,

if you will. I have two passions, Lord Illingworth: my love of him, my hate of you. You cannot kill those. They feed each other.

LORD ILLINGWORTH.   What sort of love is that which needs to have hate as its brother?

MRS ARBUTHNOT.   It is the sort of love I have for Gerald. Do you think that terrible? Well, it is terrible. All love is terrible. All love is tragedy. I loved you once, Lord Illingworth. Oh, what a tragedy for a woman to have loved you!

LORD ILLINGWORTH.   So you really refuse to marry me?

MRS ARBUTHNOT.   Yes.

LORD ILLINGWORTH.   Because you hate me?

MRS ARBUTHNOT.   Yes.

LORD ILLINGWORTH.   And does my son hate me as you do?

MRS ARBUTHNOT.   No.

LORD ILLINGWORTH.   I am glad of that, Rachel.

MRS ARBUTHNOT.   He merely despises you.

LORD ILLINGWORTH.   What a pity! What a pity for him, I mean.

MRS ARBUTHNOT.   Don't be deceived, George. Children begin by loving their parents. After a time they judge them. Rarely if ever do they forgive them.

LORD ILLINGWORTH [reads letter over again, very slowly.]
May I ask by what arguments you made the boy who
wrote this letter, this beautiful, passionate letter, believe
that you should not marry his father, the father of your
own child?

MRS ARBUTHNOT.   It was not I who made him see it.
It was another.

LORD ILLINGWORTH.   What *fin-de-siècle* person?

MRS ARBUTHNOT.   The Puritan, Lord Illingworth.
[A pause.]

LORD ILLINGWORTH [winces, then rises slowly and goes
over to the table where his hat and gloves are. Mrs Arbuthnot is
standing close to the table. He picks up one of the gloves, and
begins putting it on.] There is not much then for me to do
here, Rachel?

MRS ARBUTHNOT.   Nothing.

LORD ILLINGWORTH.   It is good-bye, is it?

MRS ARBUTHNOT.   For ever, I hope, this time, Lord
Illingworth.

LORD ILLINGWORTH.   How curious! At this moment
you look exactly as you looked the night you left me
twenty years ago. You have just the same expression in your
mouth. Upon my word, Rachel, no woman ever loved me
as you did. Why, you gave yourself to me like a flower, to
do anything I liked with. You were the prettiest of play-
things, the most fascinating of small romances ...
[Pulls out watch.] Quarter to two! Must be strolling back
to Hunstanton. Don't suppose I shall see you there again.
I'm sorry, I am, really. It's been an amusing experience to
have met amongst people of one's own rank, and treated
quite seriously too, one's mistress and one's –

[Mrs Arbuthnot snatches up glove and strikes Lord Illingworth across the face with it. Lord Illingworth starts. He is dazed by the insult of his punishment. Then he controls himself and goes to the window and looks out at his son. Sighs and leaves the room.]

MRS ARBUTHNOT *[falls sobbing on the sofa.]* He would have said it. He would have said it.
[Enter Gerald and Hester from the garden.]

GERALD. Well, dear mother. You never came out after all. So we have come in to fetch you. Mother, you have not been crying? *[Kneels down beside her.]*

MRS ARBUTHNOT. My boy! My boy! My boy!
[Running her fingers through his hair.]

HESTER *[coming over.]* But you have two children now. You'll let me be your daughter?

MRS ARBUTHNOT *[looking up.]* Would you choose me for a mother?

HESTER. You of all women I have ever known.

[They move towards the door leading into garden with their arms round each other's waists. Gerald goes to table L. C. for his hat. On turning round he sees Lord Illingworth's glove lying on the floor, and picks it up.]

GERALD. Hallo, mother, whose glove is this? You have had a visitor? Who was it?

MRS ARBUTHNOT *[turning round.]* Oh! no one. No one in particular. A man of no importance.

CURTAIN

38

An Ideal Husband - From Act 2

LADY CHILTERN *[To Lord Goring.]* Do sit down. I am so glad you have called. I want to talk to you about … well, not about bonnets, or the Woman's Liberal Association. You take far too much interest in the first subject, and not nearly enough in the second.

LORD GORING.   You want to talk to me about Mrs Cheveley?

LADY CHILTERN.   Yes. You have guessed it. After you left last night I found out what she had said was really true. Of course I made Robert write her a letter at once, withdrawing his promise.

LORD GORING.   So he gave me to understand.

LADY CHILTERN.   To have kept it would have been the first stain on a career that has been stainless always. Robert must be above reproach. He is not like other men. He cannot afford to do what other's do. *[She looks at Lord Goring, who remains silent.]* Don't you agree with me? You are Robert's greatest friend. You are our greatest friend, Lord Goring. No one, except myself, knows Robert better than you do. He has no secrets from me, and I don't think he has any from you.

LORD GORING.   He certainly has no secrets from me. At least I don't think so.

LADY CHITERN.   Then am I not right in my estimate of him? I know I am right. But speak to me frankly.

LORD GORING *[Looking straight at her.]*   Quite frankly?

LADY CHILTERN.   Surely. You have nothing to conceal, have you?

LORD GORING. Nothing. But, my dear Lady Chiltern, I think, if you will allow me to say so, that in practical life –

LADY CHILTERN [Smiling.] Of which you know so little, Lord Goring –

LORD GORING. Of which I know nothing by experience, though I know something by observation. I think that in practical life there is something about success, actual success, that is a little unscrupulous, something about ambition that is unscrupulous always. Once a man has set his heart and soul on getting to a certain point, if he has to climb the crag, he climbs the crag; if he has to walk in the mire –

LADY CHILTERN. Well?

LORD GORING. He walks in the mire. Of course I am only talking generally about life.

LADY CHILTERN [Gravely.] I hope so. Why do you look at me so strangely, Lord Goring?

LORD GORING. Lady Chiltern, I have sometimes thought that ... perhaps you are a little hard in some of your views on life. I think that ... often you don't make sufficient allowances. In every nature there are elements of weakness, or worse than weakness. Supposing, for instance, that – that any public man, my father, or Lord Meron, or Robert, say, had, years ago, written some foolish letter to some one ...

LADY CHILTERN. What do you mean by a foolish letter?

LORD GORING. A letter gravely compromising one's postion. I am only putting an imaginary case.

LADY CHILTERN. Robert is as incapable of doing a foolish thing as he is of doing a wrong thing.

LORD GORING [*After a long pause.*] Nobody is incapable of doing a foolish thing as he is of doing a wrong thing.

LADY CHILTERN. Are you a Pessimist? What will the other dandies say? They will all have to go into mourning.

LORD GORING [*Rising.*] No, Lady Chiltern, I am not a Pessimist. Indeed I am not sure that I quite know what Pessimism really means. All I do know is that life cannot be understood without much charity, cannot be lived without much charity. It is love, and not German philosophy, that is the true explanation of this world, whatever may be the explanation of the next. And if you are ever in trouble, Lady Chiltern, trust me absolutely, and I will help you in every way I can. If you ever want me, come to me for assistance, and you shall have it. Come at once to me.

LADY CHILTERN [*Looking at him in surprise.*] Lord Goring, you are talking quite seriously. I don't think I ever heard you talk seriously before.

LORD GORING [*Laughing.*] You must excuse me, Lady Chiltern. It won't occur again, if I can help it.

LADY CHILTERN. But I like you to be serious.
[*Enter Mabel Chiltern, in the most ravishing frock.*]

MABEL CHILTERN. Dear Gertrude, don't say such a dreadful thing to Lord Goring. Seriousness would be very unbecoming to him. Good afternoon, Lord Goring! Pray be as trivial as you can.

LORD GORING. I should like to, Miss Mabel, but I am afraid I am … a little out of practice this morning; and besides, I have to be going now.

MABEL CHILTERN.   Just when I have come in! What dreadful manners you have! I am sure you were very badly brought up.

LORD GORING.   I was.

MABEL CHILTERN.   I wish I had brought you up!

LORD GORING.   I am so sorry you didn't.

MABEL CHILTERN.   It is too late now, I suppose?

LORD GORING [*Smiling.*]   I am not so sure.

MABEL CHILTERN.   Will you ride tomorrow morning?

LORD GORING.   Yes, at ten.

MABEL CHILTERN.   Don't forget.

LORD GORING.   Of course I shan't. By the way, Lady Chiltern, there is no list of your guests in 'The Morning Post' of today. It has apparently been crowded out by the County Council, or the Lambeth Conference, or something equally boring. Could you let me have a list? I have a particular reason for asking you.

LADY CHILTERN.   I am sure Mr Trafford will be able to give you one.

LORD GORING.   Thanks, so much.

MABEL CHILTERN.   Tommy is the most useful person in London.

LORD GORING [*Turning to her.*]   And who is the most ornamental?

MABEL CHILTERN [*Triumphantly.*]   I am.

LORD GORING. How clever of you to guess it! *[Takes up his hat and cane.]* Goodbye, Lady Chiltern! You will remember what I said to you, won't you?

LADY CHILTERN. Yes; but I don't know why you said it to me.

LORD GORING. I hardly know myself. Goodbye, Miss Mabel!

MABEL CHILTERN *[With a little moue of disappointment.]* I wish you were not going. I have had four wonderful adventures this morning; four and a half, in fact. You might stop and listen to some of them.

LORD GORING. How very selfish of you to have four and a half! There won't be any left for me.

MABEL CHILTERN. I don't want you to have any. They would not be good for you.

LORD GORING. That is the first unkind thing you have ever said to me. How charmingly you said it!
Ten tomorrow.

MABEL CHILTERN. Sharp.

LORD GORING. Quite sharp. But don't bring Mr Trafford.

MABEL CHILTERN *[With a little toss of the head.]* Of course I shan't bring Tommy Trafford. Tommy Trafford is in great disgrace.

LORD GORING. I am delighted to hear it.

[Bows and goes out.]

An Ideal Husband - From Act 2

MRS CHEVELEY.   Wonderful woman, Lady Markby, isn't she? Talks more and says less than anybody I ever met. She is made to be a public speaker. Much more so than her husband, though he is a typical Englishman, always dull and usually violent.

LADY CHILTERN *[Makes no answer but remains standing. There is a pause. Then the eyes of the two women meet. Lady Chiltern looks stern and pale. Mrs Cheveley seems rather amused.]* Mrs Cheveley, I think it is right to tell you quite frankly that, had I known who you really were, I should not have invited you to my house last night.

MRS CHEVELEY *[With an impertinent smile.]*   Really?

LADY CHILTERN.   I could not have done so.

MRS CHEVELEY.   I see that after all these years you have not changed a bit, Gertrude.

LADY CHILTERN.   I never change.

MRS CHEVELEY *[Elevating her eyebrows.]*   Then life has taught you nothing?

LADY CHILTERN.   It has taught me that a person who has once been guilty of a dishonest and dishonourable action may be guilty of it a second time, and should be shunned.

MRS CHEVELEY.   Would you apply that rule to everyone?

LADY CHILTERN.   Yes, to everyone, without exception.

MRS CHEVELEY.   Then, I am sorry for you Gertrude, very sorry for you.

LADY CHILTERN. You see now, I am sure, that for
many reasons any further acquaintance between us during
your stay in London is quite impossible?

MRS CHEVELEY *[Leaning back in her chair.]* Do you
know, Gertrude, I don't mind your talking morality a bit.
Morality is simply the attitude we adopt towards people
whom we personally dislike. You dislike me. I am quite
aware of that. And I have always detested you. And yet I
have come here to do you a service.

LADY CHILTERN *[Contemptuously.]* Like the service
you wished to render my husband last night, I suppose.
Thank heaven, I saved him from that.

MRS CHEVELEY *[Starting to her feet.]* It was you who
made him write that indolent letter to me? It was you
who made him break his promise?

LADY CHILTERN. Yes.

MRS CHEVELEY. Then you must make him keep it. I
give you till tomorrow morning – no more. If by that
time your husband does not solemnly bind himself to help
me in this great scheme in which I am interested –

LADY CHILTERN. This fraudulent speculation –

MRS CHEVELEY. Call it what you choose. I hold your
husband in the hollow of my hand, and if you are wise you
will make him do what I tell him.

LADY CHILTERN *[Rising and going towards her.]* You are
impertinent. What has my husband to do with you? With a
woman like you?

MRS CHEVELEY *[With a bitter laugh.]* In this world like
meets with like. It is because your husband is himself

fraudulent and dishonest that we pair so well together. Between you and him there are chasms. He and I are closer than friends. We are enemies linked together. The same sin binds us.

LADY CHILTERN.   How dare you class my husband with yourself? How dare you threaten him or me? Leave my house. You are unfit to enter it.

[Sir Robert Chiltern enters from behind. He hears his wife's last words, and sees to whom they are addressed. He grows deadly pale.]

MRS CHEVELEY.   Your house! A house bought with the price of dishonour. A house, everything in which has been paid for by fraud. [Turns round and sees Sir Robert Chiltern.] Ask him what the origin of his fortune is! Get him to tell you how he sold to a stockbroker a Cabinet secret. Learn from him to what you owe your position.

LADY CHILTERN.   It is not true! Robert! It is not true!

MRS CHEVELEY [Pointing at him with outstretched finger.] Look at him! Can he deny it? Does he dare to?

SIR ROBERT CHILTERN.   Go! Go at once. You have done your worst now.

MRS CHEVELEY.   My worst? I have not yet finished with you, with either of you. I give you both till tomorrow at noon. If by then you don't do what I bid you to do, the whole world shall know the origin of Robert Chiltern.

[Sir Robert Chiltern strikes the bell. Enter Mason.]

SIR ROBERT CHILTERN.   Show Mrs Cheveley out.

[Mrs Cheveley starts; then bows with somewhat exaggerated politeness to Lady Chiltern, who makes no sign of response. As she passes by Sir Robert Chiltern, who is standing close to the door, she pauses for a moment and looks him straight in the face. She then goes out, followed by the servant, who closes the door after him. The husband and wife are left alone. Lady Chiltern stands like someone in a dreadful dream. Then she turns round and looks at her husband. She looks at him with strange eyes, as though she was seeing him for the first time.]

LADY CHILTERN. You sold a Cabinet secret for money! You began your life with fraud! You built up a career on dishonour! Oh, tell me it is not true! Lie to me! Tell me it is not true!

SIR ROBERT CHILTERN. What this woman said is quite true. But, Gertrude, listen to me. You don't realize how I was tempted. Let me tell you the whole thing. *[Goes towards her.]*

LADY CHILTERN. Don't come near me. Don't touch me. I feel as if you had soiled me for ever. Oh! what a mask you have been wearing all these years! A horrible painted mask! You sold yourself for money. Oh! a common thief were better. You put yourself up for sale to the highest bidder! You were bought in the market. You lied to the whole world. And yet you will not lie to me.

SIR ROBERT CHILTERN *[Rushing towards her.]* Gertrude! Gertrude!

LADY CHILTERN *[Thrusting him back with outstretched hands.]* No, don't speak! Say nothing! Your voice wakes terrible memories – memories of things that made me love you – memories of words that made me love you – memories that now are horrible to me. And how I worshipped you! You were to me something apart from common life, a thing pure, noble, honest, without stain.

The world seemed to me finer because you were in it, and goodness more real because you lived. And now – oh, when I think that I made of a man like you my ideal! the ideal of my life!

SIR ROBERT CHILTERN.   There was your mistake. There was your error. The error all women commit. Why can't you women love us, faults and all? Why do you place us on monstrous pedestals? We have all feet of clay, women as well as men; but when we men love women, we love them knowing their weaknesses, their follies, their imperfections, love them all the more, it may be, for that reason. It is not the perfect, but the imperfect, who have need of love. It is when we are wounded by our own hands, or by the hands of others, that love should come to cure us – else what use is love at all? All sins, except a sin against itself, Love should forgive. All lives, save loveless lives, true Love should pardon. A man's love is like that. It is wider, larger, more human than a woman's. Women think that they are making ideals of men. What they are making of us are false idols merely. You made your false idol of me, and I had not the courage to come down, to show you my wounds, tell you my weaknesses. I was afraid that I might lose your love, as I have lost it now. And so, last night you ruined my life for me – yes, ruined it! What this woman asked of me was nothing compared to what she offered to me. She offered security, peace, stability. The sin of my youth, that I had thought was buried, rose up in front of me, hideous, horrible, with its hands at my throat. I could have killed it for ever, sent it back into its tomb, destroyed its record, burned the one witness against me. You prevented me. No one but you, you know it. And now what is there before me but public disgrace, ruin, terrible shame, the mockery of the world, a lonely dishonoured life, a lonely dishonoured death, it may be, some day? Let women make no more ideals of men! let them not put them on altars and bow before them, or they may ruin other lives as completely as you – you whom I have so wildly loved – have ruined mine!

[He passes from the room. Lady Chiltern rushes towards him, but the door is closed when she reaches it. Pale with anguish, bewildered, helpless, she sways like a plant in the water. Her hands, outstretched, seem to tremble in the air like blossoms in the wind. Then she flings herself down beside a sofa and buries her face. Her sobs are like the sobs of a child.]

ACT DROP

The Importance Of Being Earnest – From Act 2

CECILY.   My dear guardian, with the assistance of Miss Prism, has the arduous task of looking after me.

GWENDOLEN.   Your guardian?

CECILY.   Yes, I am Mr Worthing's ward.

GWENDOLEN.   It is strange he never mentioned to me that he had a ward. How secretive of him! He grows more interesting hourly. I am not sure, however, that the news inspires me with feelings of unmixed delight. *[Rising and going to her.]* I am very fond of you, Cecily; I have liked you ever since I met you! But I am bound to state that now I know that you are Mr Worthing's ward, I cannot help expressing a wish you were – well just a little older than you seemed to be – and not quite so very alluring in appearance. In fact, if I may speak candidly –

CECILY. Pray do! I think that whenever one has anything unpleasant to say, one should always be quite candid.

GWENDOLEN.   Well, to speak with perfect candour, Cecily, I wish that you were fully forty-two, and more than usually plain for your age. Ernest has a strong upright nature. He is the very soul of truth and honour. Disloyalty would be as impossible to him as deception. But even men of the noblest possible moral character are extremely susceptible to the influence of the physical charms of others. Modern, no less than Ancient History, supplies us with many most painful examples of what I refer to. If it were not so, indeed, History would be quite unreadable.

CECILY.   I beg your pardon, Gwendolen, did you say Ernest?

GWENDOLEN.   Yes.

CECILY.   Oh, but it is not Mr Ernest Worthing who is my guardian. It is his brother – his eldest brother.

GWENDOLEN *[Sitting down again.)*   Ernest never mentioned to me that he had a brother.

CECILY.   I am sorry to say that they have not been on good terms for a long time.

GWENDOLEN.   Ah! that accounts for it. And now that I think of it I have never heard any man mention his brother. The subject seems distasteful to most men. Cecily, you have lifted a load from my mind. I was growing almost anxious. It would have been terrible if any cloud had come across a friendship like ours, would it not? Of course you are quite, quite sure that it is not Mr Ernest Worthing who is your guardian?

CECILY.   Quite sure. *[A pause.]* In fact, I am going to be his.

GWENDOLEN *[Enquiringly.]*   I beg your pardon?

CECILY *[Rather shy and confidingly.]*   Dearest Gwendolen, there is no reason why I should make a secret of it to you. Our little county newspaper is sure to chronicle the fact next week. Mr Ernest Worthing and I are engaged to be married.

GWENDOLEN [Quite politely, rising.]   My darling Cecily, I think there must be some slight error. Mr Ernest Worthing is engaged to me. The announcement will appear in the 'Morning Post' on Saturday at the latest.

CECILY [Very politely, rising.)   I am afraid you must be under some misconception. Ernest proposed to me exactly ten minutes ago.

[Shows diary.]

GWENDOLEN [Examines diary through her lorgnette carefully.]   It is certainly very curious, for he asked me to be his wife yesterday afternoon at 5.30. If you would care to verify the incident, pray do so. [Produces diary of her own.]   I never travel without my diary. One should always have something sensational to read in the train.   I am so sorry, dear Cecily, if it is any disappointment to you, but I am afraid I have the prior claim.

CECILY.   It would distress me more than I can tell you, dear Gwendolen, if it caused you any mental or physical anguish, but I feel bound to point out that since Ernest proposed to you he clearly has changed his mind.

GWENDOLEN [Meditatively.]   If the poor fellow has been entrapped into any foolish promise I shall consider it my duty to rescue him at once, and with a firm hand.

CECILY [Thoughtfully and sadly.)   Whatever the unfortunate entanglement my dear boy may have got into, I will never reproach him with it after we are married.

GWENDOLEN.   Do you allude to me, Miss Cardew, as an entanglement? You are presumptuous. On an occasion of this kind it becomes more than a moral duty to speak one's mind. It becomes a pleasure.

CECILY. Do you suggest, Miss Fairfax, that I entrapped Ernest into an engagement? How dare you? This is no time for wearing the shallow mask of manners. When I see a spade I call it a spade.

GWENDOLEN [Satirically.] I am glad to say that I have never seen a spade. It is obvious that our social spheres have been widely different.

[Enter Merriman, followed by the footman. He carries a salver, table cloth, and plate stand. Cecily is about to retort. The presence of the servants exercises a restraining influence, under which both girls chafe.]

MERRIMAN. Shall I lay tea here as usual, Miss?

CECILY [Sternly, in a calm voice.] Yes, as usual.

[Merriman begins to clear table and lay cloth. A long pause. Cecily and Gwendolen glare at each other.]

GWENDOLEN. Are there many interesting walks in the vicinity, Miss Cardew?

CECILY. Oh yes! a great many. From the top of one of the hills quite close one can see five counties.

GWENDOLEN. Five counties! I don't think I should like that. I hate crowds.

CECILY [Sweetly.] I suppose that is why you live in a town?

[Gwendolen bites her lip, and beats her foot nervously with her parasol.]

GWENDOLEN [Looking around.] Quite a well-kept garden this is, Miss Cardew.

CECILY. So glad you like it, Miss Fairfax.

GWENDOLEN. I had no idea there were any flowers in the country.

CECILY. Oh, flowers are as common here, Miss Fairfax, as people are in London.

GWENDOLEN. Personally, I cannot understand how anybody manages to exist in the country, if anybody who is anybody does. The country always bores me to death.

CECILY. Ah! This is what the newspapers call agricultural depression, is it not? I believe the aristocracy are suffering very much from it just at present. It is almost epidemic amongst them, I have been told. May I offer you some tea, Miss Fairfax?

GWENDOLEN *[With elaborate politeness.]* Thank you. *[Aside.]* Detestable girl! But I require tea!

CECILY *[Sweetly.]* Sugar?

GWENDOLEN *[Superciliously.]* No, thank you. Sugar is not fashionable any more.

[Cecily looks angrily at her, takes up the tongs and puts four lumps of sugar into the cup.]

CECILY *[Severely.]* Cake or bread and butter?

GWENDOLEN *[In a bored manner.]* Bread and butter, please. Cake is rarely seen at the best houses nowadays.

CECILY *[Cuts a very large slice of cake, and puts it on the tray.]* Hand that to Miss Fairfax.

*[Merriman does so, and goes with the footman. Gwendolen
drinks the tea and makes a grimace. Puts down cup at once,
reaches out her hand to the bread and butter, looks at it, and
finds it is cake. Rises in indignation.]*

GWENDOLEN. You have filled my tea with lumps of
sugar, and though I asked most distinctly for bread and
butter, you have given me cake. I am known for the
gentleness of my disposition, and the extraordinary
sweetness of my nature, but I warn you, Miss Cardew, you
may go too far.

CECILY *[Rising.]* To save my poor, innocent, trusting boy
from the machinations of any other girl, there are no
lengths to which I would not go.

GWENDOLEN. From the moment I saw you I distrusted
you. I felt that you were false and deceitful. I am never
deceived in such matters. My first impressions of people
are invariably right.

CECILY.   It seems to me, Miss Fairfax, that I am
trespassing on your valuable time. No doubt you have
other calls of a similar character to make in the
neighbourhood.

[Enter Jack.]

GWENDOLEN *[Catching sight of him.]* Ernest! My own
Ernest!

JACK. Gwendolen! Darling! *[Offers to kiss her.]*

GWENDOLEN *[Drawing back.]* A moment! May I ask if
you are engaged to be married to this young lady?
[Points to Cecily.]

JACK [Laughing.] To dear little Cecily! Of course not! What could have put such an idea into your pretty little head?

GWENDOLEN. Thank you. You may! [Offers her cheek.]

CECILY [Very sweetly.] I knew there must be some misunderstanding, Miss Fairfax. The gentleman whose arm is at present round your waist is my dear guardian, Mr John Worthing.

GWENDOLEN. I beg your pardon?

CECILY. This is Uncle Jack.

GWENDOLEN [Receding.] Jack! Oh!

[Enter Algernon.]

CECILY. Here is Ernest.

ALGERNON [Goes straight over to Cecily without noticing anyone else.] My own love! [Offers to kiss her.]

CECILY [Drawing back.) A moment, Ernest! May I ask you – are you engaged to be married to this young lady?

ALGERNON [Looking round.] To what young lady? Good heavens! Gwendolen!

CECILY. Yes, to good heavens, Gwendolen, I mean to Gwendolen.

ALGERNON [Laughing.] Of course not! What could have put such an idea into your pretty little head?

CECILY. Thank you. [Presenting her cheek to be kissed.] You may.

[Algernon kisses her.]

GWENDOLEN.   I felt sure there was some slight error, Miss Cardew. The gentleman who is now embracing you is my cousin, Mr Algernon Moncrieff.

CECILY *[Breaking away from Algernon.]*   Algernon Moncrieff! Oh!

The Importance Of Being Earnest – From Act 3

LADY BRACKNELL *[Starting.]*   Miss Prism! Did I hear you mention a Miss Prism?

CHASUBLE.   Yes, Lady Bracknell. I am on my way to join her.

LADY BRACKNELL.   Pray allow me to detain you for a moment. This matter may prove to be one of vital importance to Lord Bracknell and myself. Is this Miss Prism a female of repellent aspect, remotely connected with education?

CHASUBLE *[Somewhat indignantly.]*   She is the most cultivated of ladies and the very picture of respectability.

LADY BRACKNELL.   It is obviously the same person. May I ask what position she holds in your household?

CHASUBLE *[Severely.]*   I am a celibate, madam.

JACK *[Interposing.]*   Miss Prism, Lady Bracknell, has been for the last three years Miss Cardew's esteemed governess and valued companion.

LADY BRACKNELL.   In spite of what I hear of her, I must see her at once. Let her be sent for.

CHASUBLE [Looking off.]   She approaches; she is nigh.

[Enter Miss Prism hurriedly.]

MISS PRISM.   I was told you expected me in the vestry, dear Canon. I have been waiting for you there for an hour and three quarters. [Catches sight of Lady Bracknell who has fixed her with a stormy stare. Miss Prism grows pale and quails. She looks anxiously round as if desirous to escape.]

LADY BRACKNELL [In a severe judicial voice.]   Prism! [Miss Prism bows her head in shame.] Come here, Prism! [Miss Prism approaches in a humble manner.] Prism! Where is that baby? [General consternation. The Canon starts back in horror. Algernon and Jack pretend to be anxious to shield Cecily and Gwendolen from hearing the details of a terrible public scandal.] Twenty-eight years ago, Prism, you left Lord Bracknell's house, Number 104, Upper Grosvenor Street, in charge of a perambulator that contained a baby, of the male sex. You never returned. A few weeks later, through the elaborate investigations of the Metropolitan police, the perambulator was discovered at midnight, standing by itself in a remote corner of Bayswater. It contained the manuscript of a three-volume novel of more than usually revolting sentimentality. [Miss Prism starts in involuntary indignation.] But the baby was not there! [Everyone looks at Miss Prism.]   Prism! Where is that baby? [A pause.]

MISS PRISM.   Lady Bracknell, I admit with shame that I do not know. I only wish I did. The plain facts of the case are these. On the morning of the day you mention, a day that is for ever branded on my memory, I prepared as usual to take the baby out in its perambulator. I had also with me a somewhat old, but capricious handbag in which I had intended to place the manuscript of a work of fiction that I had written during my few unoccupied hours. In a moment of mental abstraction, for which I can never forgive myself, I deposited the manuscript in the bassinette, and placed the baby in the hand-bag.

JACK [Who has been listening attentively.]   But where did you deposit the hand-bag?

MISS PRISM.   Do not ask me, Mr Worthing.

JACK.   Miss Prism, this is a matter of no small importance to me. I insist on knowing where you deposited the hand-bag that contained that infant.

MISS PRISM.   I left it in the cloak-room of one of the larger railway stations in London.

JACK.   What railway station?

MISS PRISM [Quite crushed.]   Victoria. The Brighton line. [Sinks into a chair.]

JACK.   I must retire to my room for a moment. Gwendolen, wait here for me.

GWENDOLEN.   If you are not too long, I will wait here for you all my life.

[Exit Jack in great excitement.]

CHASUBLE.   What do you think this means, Lady Bracknell?

LADY BRACKNELL.   I dare not even suspect, Dr Chasuble. I need hardly tell you that in families of high position strange coincidences are not supposed to occur. They are hardly considered the thing.

[Noises heard overhead as if someone was throwing trunks around. Everyone looks up.]

CECILY.   Uncle Jack seems strangely agitated.

CHASUBLE.   Your guardian has a very emotional nature.

LADY BRACKNELL.   This noise is extremely unpleasant. It sounds as if he was having an argument. I dislike arguments of any kind. They are always vulgar, and often convincing.

CHASUBLE *[Looking up.]*   It has stopped now. *[The noise is redoubled.]*

LADY BRACKNELL.   I wish he would arrive at some conclusion.

GWENDOLEN.   This suspense is terrible. I hope it will last.

[Enter Jack with a hand-bag of black leather in his hand.]

JACK *[Rushing over to Miss Prism.]*   Is this the hand-bag, Miss Prism? Examine it carefully before you speak. The happiness of more than one life depends on your answer.

MISS PRISM *[Calmly.]*   It seems to be mine. Yes, here is the injury it received through the upsetting of a Gower Street omnibus in younger and happier days. Here is the stain on the lining caused by the explosion of a temperence beverage, an incident that occurred at Leamington. And here, on the lock, are my initials. I had forgotten that in an extravagant mood I had had them placed there. The bag is undoubtedly mine. I am delighted to have it so unexpectedly restored to me. It has been a great inconvenience being without it all these years.

JACK *[In a pathetic voice.]*   Miss Prism, more is restored to you than this hand-bag. I was the baby you placed in it.

MISS PRISM [*Amazed.*]   You?

JACK [*Embracing her.*]   Yes ... mother!

MISS PRISM [*Recoiling in indignant astonishment.*]
Mr Worthing! I am unmarried!

JACK.   Unmarried! I do not deny that is a serious blow.
But after all, who has the right to cast a stone against
anyone who has suffered? Cannot repentance wipe out an
act of folly? Why should there be one law for men, and
another for women? Mother, I forgive you. [*Tries to embrace
her again.*]

MISS PRISM [*Still more indignant.*]   Mr Worthing, there is
some error. [*Pointing to Lady Bracknell.*] There is the lady
who can tell you who you really are.

JACK [*After a pause.*]   Lady Bracknell, I hate to seem
inquisitive, but would you kindly inform me who I am?

LADY BRACKNELL.   I am afraid that the news I have to
give you will not altogether please you. You are the son of
my poor sister, Mrs Moncrieff, and consequently
Algernon's elder brother.

JACK.   Algy's elder brother! Then I have a brother after
all. I knew I had a brother! I always said I had a brother!
Cecily – how could you have ever doubted that I had a
brother. [*Seizes hold of Algernon.*] Dr Chasuble, my
unfortunate brother. Miss Prism, my unfortunate brother.
Gwendolen, my unfortunate brother. Algy, you young
scoundrel, you will have to treat me with more respect in
the future. You have never behaved to me like a brother in
all your life.

ALGERNON.   Well, not till today, old boy, I admit. I did
my best, however, though I was out of practice. [*Shakes
hands.*]

GWENDOLEN [*To Jack.*]   My own! But what own are you? What is your Christian name, now that you have become someone else?

JACK.   Good heavens! ... I had quite forgotten that point. Your decision on the subject of my name is irrevocable, I suppose?

GWENDOLEN.   I never change, except in my affections.

CECILY.   What a noble nature you have, Gwendolen!

JACK.   Then, the question had better be cleared up at once. Aunt Augusta, a moment. At the time when Miss Prism left me in the handbag, had I been christened already?

LADY BRACKNELL.   Every luxury that money could buy, including christening, had been lavished on you by your fond and doting parents.

JACK.   Then I was christened! That is settled. Now, what name was I given? Let me know the worst.

LADY BRACKNELL.   Being the eldest son you were naturally christened after your father.

JACK [*Irritably.*]   Yes, but what was my father's Christian name?

LADY BRACKNELL [*Meditatively.*]   I cannot at the present moment recall what the General's Christian name was. But I have no doubt that he had one. He was eccentric, I admit. But only in later years. And that was the result of the Indian climate, and marriage, and indigestion, and other things of that kind.

JACK.   Algy! Can't you recollect what our father's Christian name was?

ALGERNON.   My dear boy, we were never even on speaking terms. He died before I was a year old.

JACK.   His name would appear in the Army lists of the period, I suppose, Aunt Augusta?

LADY BRACKNELL.   The General was essentially a man of peace, except in his domestic life. But I have no doubt his name would appear in any military directory.

JACK.   The Army Lists of the last forty years are here. These delightful records should have been my constant study. *[Rushes to bookcase and tears the books out.]* M. Generals … Mallam, Migsby, Mobbs, Moncrieff! Lieutenant 1840, Captain Lieutenant-Colonel, Colonel, General 1869, Christian names, Ernest John. *[Puts book very quietly down and speaks quite calmly.]* I always told you, Gwendolen, my name was Ernest, didn't I? Well, it is Ernest after all. I mean it naturally is Ernest.

LADY BRACKNELL.   Yes, I remember now that the General was called Ernest. I knew I had some particular reason for disliking the name.

GWENDOLEN.   Ernest! My own Ernest! I felt from the first that you could have no other name!

JACK.   Gwendolen, it is a terrible thing for a man to find out suddenly that all his life he has been speaking nothing but the truth. Can you forgive me?

GWENDOLEN.   I can. For I feel that you are sure to change.

JACK.   My own one!

CHASUBLE *[To Miss Prism.]*   Lætitia! *[Embraces her.]*

MISS PRISM [*Enthusiastically.*]   Frederick! At last!

ALGERNON.   Cecily! [*Embraces her.*] At last!

JACK.   Gwendolen! [*Embraces her.*] At last!

LADY BRACKNELL.   My nephew, you seem to be displaying signs of triviality.

JACK.   On the contrary, Aunt Augusta, I've now realized for the first time in my life the vital importance of being Earnest.

CURTAIN

The Happy Prince

High above the city, on a tall column, stood a statue of the
Happy Prince. He was gilded with thin leaves of fine gold,
for eyes he had two bright sapphires, and a large red ruby
glowed on his sword-hilt.

He was very much admired indeed. 'He is as beautiful as a
weathercock,' remarked one of the Town Councillors who
wished to gain a reputation for having artistic tastes; 'only
not quite so useful', he added, fearing lest people should
think him unpractical, which he really was not.

'Why can't you be like the Happy Prince?' asked a sensible
mother of her little boy who was crying for the moon.
'The Happy Prince never dreams of crying for anything.'
'I am glad there is some one in the world who is quite
happy,' muttered a disappointed man as he gazed at the
wonderful statue.

'He looks just like an angel', said the Charity Children as
they came out of the cathedral in their bright scarlet
cloaks, and their clean white pinafores.

'How do you know?' said the Mathematical Master, 'you
have never seen one.'

'Ah! but we have, in our dreams,' answered the children;
and the Mathematical Master frowned and looked very
severe, for he did not approve of children dreaming. One
night there flew over the city a little Swallow. His friends
had gone away to Egypt six weeks before, but he had
stayed behind, for he was in love with the most beautiful
Reed. He had just met her early in the spring as he was
flying down the river after a big yellow moth, and had
been so attracted by her slender waist that he had stopped
to talk to her.

'Shall I love you?' said the Swallow, who liked to come to the point at once, and the Reed made him a low bow. So he flew round and round her, touching the water with his wings, and making silver ripples. This was his courtship, and it lasted all through the summer.

'It's a ridiculous attachment,' twittered the other Swallows, 'she has no money, and far too many relations;' and indeed the river was quite full of Reeds. Then, when the autumn came, they all flew away.

After they had gone he felt lonely, and began to tire of his lady-love. 'She has no conversation', he said, 'and I am afraid that she is a coquette, for she is always flirting with the wind.' And certainly, whenever the wind blew, the Reed made the most grateful curtsies. 'I admit that she is domestic', he continued, 'but I love travelling, and my wife, consequently, should love travelling also'.

'Will you come away with me?' he said finally to her; but the Reed shook her head, she was so attached to her home. 'You have been trifling with me', he cried, 'I am off to the Pyramids. Goodbye!' and he flew away.

All day long he flew, and at night-time he arrived at the city. 'Where shall I put up?' he said; 'I hope the town has made preparations.'

Then he saw the statue on the tall column. 'I will put up there,' he cried; 'it is a fine position with plenty of fresh air.' So he alighted just between the feet of the Happy Prince.

'I have a golden bedroom,' he said softly to himself as he looked round, and he prepared to go to sleep; but just as he was putting his head under his wing a large drop of water fell on him. 'What a curious thing!' he cried, 'there is not a single cloud in the sky, the stars are quite clear and

So the Swallow picked out the great ruby from the Prince's sword, and flew away with it in his beak over the roofs of the town.

He passed by the cathedral tower, where the white marble angels were sculptured. He passed by the palace and heard the sound of dancing. A beautiful girl came out on the balcony with her lover. 'How wonderful the stars are,' he said to her, 'and how wonderful is the power of love!'

'I hope my dress will be ready in time for the State-ball,' she answered; 'I have ordered passion-flowers to be embroidered on it; but the seamstresses are so lazy.'

He passed over the river, and saw the lanterns hanging to the masts of the ships. He passed over the Ghetto, and saw the old Jews bargaining with each other, and weighing out money in copper scales. At last he came to the poor house and looked in. The boy was tossing feverishly on his bed, and the mother had fallen asleep, she was so tired. In he hopped, and laid the great ruby on the table beside the woman's thimble. Then he flew gently round the bed, fanning the boy's forehead with his wings.

'How cool I feel,' said the boy, 'I must be getting better;' and he sank into a delicious slumber.

Then the Swallow flew back to the Happy Prince, and told him what he had done. 'It is curious,' he remarked, 'but I feel quite warm now, although it is so cold.'

'That is because you have done a good action,' said the Prince. And the little Swallow began to think, and then he fell asleep. Thinking always made him sleepy.

When day broke he flew down to the river and had a bath. 'What a remarkable phenomenon,' said the Professor of

Ornithology as he was passing over the bridge. 'A swallow in winter!' And he wrote a long letter about it to the local newspaper. Every one quoted it, it was full of so many words that they could not understand.

'Tonight I go to Egypt,' said the Swallow, and he was in high spirits at the prospect. He visited all the public monuments, and sat a long time on top of the church steeple. Wherever he went the Sparrows chirruped, and said to each other, 'What a distinguished stranger!' so he enjoyed himself very much.

When the moon rose he flew back to the Happy Prince. 'Have you any commissions for Egypt?' he cried; 'I am just starting.'

'Swallow, Swallow, little Swallow,' said the Prince, 'will you not stay with me one night longer?'

'I am waited for in Egypt,' answered the Swallow. 'Tomorrow my friends will fly up to the Second Cataract. The river-horse couches there among the bulrushes, and on a great granite throne sits the God Memnon. All night long he watches the stars, and when the morning star shines he utters one cry of joy, and then he is silent. At noon the yellow lions come down to the water's edge to drink. They have eyes like green beryls, and their roar is louder than the roar of the cataract'.

'Swallow, Swallow, little Swallow,' said the Prince, 'far away across the city I see a young man in a garret. He is leaning over a desk covered with papers, and in a tumbler by his side there is a bunch of withered violets. His hair is brown and crisp, and his lips are red as a pomegranate, and he has large and dreamy eyes. He is trying to finish a play for the Director of the Theatre, but he is too cold to write any more. There is no fire in the grate, and hunger has made him faint.'

'No, little Swallow,' said the poor Prince, 'you must go away to Egypt.'

'I will stay with you always,' said the Swallow, and he slept at the Prince's feet.

All the next day he sat on the Prince's shoulder, and told him stories of what he has seen in strange lands. He told him of the red ibises, who stand in long rows on the banks of the Nile, and catch gold fish in their beaks; of the Sphinx, who is as old as the world itself, and lives in the desert, and knows everything; of the merchants, who walk slowly by the side of their camels, and carry amber beads in their hands; of the King of the Mountains of the Moon, who is as black as ebony, and worships a large crystal; of the great green snake that sleeps in a palm-tree, and has twenty priests to feed it with honey-cakes; and of the pygmies who sail over a big lake on large flat leaves, and are always at war with the butterflies.

'Dear little Swallow,' said the Prince, 'you tell me of marvellous things, but more marvellous than anything is the suffering of men and of women. There is no Mystery so great as Misery. Fly over my city, little Swallow, and tell me what you see there.'

So the Swallow flew over the great city, and saw the rich making merry in their beautiful houses, while the beggars were sitting at the gates. He flew into dark lanes, and saw the white faces of starving children looking out listlessly at the black streets. Under the archway of a bridge two little boys were lying in one another's arms to try and keep themselves warm. 'How hungry we are!' they said. 'You must not lie here,' shouted the Watchman, and they wandered out into the rain.

Then he flew back and told the Prince what he had seen. 'I am covered with fine gold,' said the Prince, 'you must take it off, leaf by leaf, and give it to my poor; the living always think that gold can make them happy.'

Leaf after leaf of the fine gold the Swallow picked off, till the Happy Prince looked quite dull and grey. Leaf after leaf of the fine gold he brought to the poor, and the children's faces grew rosier, and they laughed and played games in the street.

'We have bread now!' they cried.

Then the snow came, and after the snow came the frost. The streets looked as if they were made of silver, they were so bright and glistening; long icicles like crystal daggers hung down from the eaves of the houses, everybody went about in furs, and the little boys wore scarlet caps and skated on the ice.

The poor little Swallow grew colder and colder, but he would not leave the Prince, he loved him too well. He picked up crumbs outside the baker's door when the baker was not looking, and tried to keep himself warm by flapping his wings.

But at last he knew that he was going to die. He had just strength to fly up to the Prince's shoulder once more.

'Goodbye, dear Prince!' he murmured, 'will you let me kiss your hand?'

'I am glad that you are going to Egypt at last, little Swallow,' said the Prince, 'you have stayed too long here; but you must kiss me on the lips, for I love you.' 'It is not to Egypt that I am going,' said the Swallow. 'I am going to the House of Death. Death is the brother of Sleep, is he not?'

And he kissed the Happy Prince on the lips, and fell down dead at his feet. At that moment a curious crack sounded

Wilde's Quotations

Action

Action! What is action? It dies at the moment of its energy.
It is a base concession to fact.

The Decay of Living

Advice

I always pass on good advice. It is the only thing to do
with it. It is never of use to oneself.

An Ideal Husband

Age

Thirty-five is a very attractive age. London society is full
of women of the very highest birth who have, of their own
free choice, remained thirty-five for years.

The Importance of Being Earnest

One should never trust a woman who tells one her real
age. A woman who would tell one that would tell one
anything.

A Woman of No Importance

Ambition

If I can produce even one more beautiful work of art I
shall be able to rob malice of its venom, and cowardice of
its sneer, and to pluck out the tongue of scorn by the
roots.

De Profundis

America and Americans

The youth of America is their oldest tradition. It has been
going on now for three hundred years. To hear them talk

one would imagine they were in their first childhood. As far as civilisation goes they are in their second.

All Americans lecture, I believe. I suppose it is something in their climate.

A Woman of No Importance

The crude commercialism of America, its materializing spirit, its indifference to the poetical side of things, and its lack of imagination and of high unattainable ideals, are entirely due to that country having adopted for its national hero a man, who according to his own confession, was incapable of telling a lie.

Lord Savile's Crime

Arguments

I dislike arguments of any kind. They are always vulgar, and often convincing.

The Importance of Being Earnest

Art

If something cannot be done to check, or at least modify, our monstrous worship of facts, Art will become sterile, and Beauty will pass away from the land.

The Decay of Living

Art does not hurt us. The tears that we shed at a play are a type of the exquisite sterile emotions that is the function of Art to awaken. We weep, but we are not wounded. We grieve, but our grief is not bitter.

The Critic as Artist

Bachelors

It's perfectly scandalous the amount of bachelors who are going about society. There should be a law passed to compel them all to marry within twelve months.

A Woman of No Importance

Fool

Remember that the fool in the eyes of the gods and the fool in the eyes of man are very different.

The real fool, such as the gods mock or mar, is he who does not know himself.

De Profundis

Foxhunting

The English country gentleman galloping after a fox – the unspeakable in full pursuit of the uneatable.

A Woman of No Importance

French Revolution

To be born, or at any rate bred, in a hand-bag, whether it had handles or not, seems to me to display a contempt for the ordinary decencies of family life that reminds one of the worst excesses of the French Revolution.

The Importance of Being Earnest

Friendship

An acquaintance that begins with a compliment is sure to develop into a real friendship. It starts in the right manner.

An Ideal Husband

Friendship is so much more tragic than love. It lasts longer.

A Few Maxims for the Instruction of the Over-Educated

God

God's house is the only house where sinners are made welcome.

God's law is only Love.

A Woman of No Importance

Hope

Nothing should be out of the reach of hope. Life is a hope.
A Woman of No Importance

House of Commons

The House of Commons really does very little harm. You can't make people good by Act of Parliament.
A Woman of No Importance

Ignorance

Ignorance is like a delicate exotic fruit; touch it and the bloom is gone.
The Importance of Being Earnest

Impartiality

It is only about things that do not interest one that one can give a really unbiased opinion, which is no doubt the reason why an unbiased opinion is always absolutely valueless.

The man who sees both side of a question, is a man who sees absolutely nothing at all.
The Critic as Artist

Intellect

To expect the unexpected shows a thoroughly modern intellect.
An Ideal Husband

Journalism

There is much to be said in favour of modern journalism. By giving us the opinions of the uneducated, it keeps us in touch with the ignorance of the community. By carefully chronicling the current events of contemporary life, it shows us what very little importance such events really are.

Some limitation might well, and will soon, I hope, be placed upon some of our newspapers and newspaper writers. For they give us the bald, sordid, disgusting facts of life.

The Critic as Artist

Kiss

A kiss may ruin a human life.

A Woman of No Importance

Life

Actors are so fortunate. They can choose whether they will appear in tragedy or comedy, whether they will suffer or make merry, laugh or shed tears. But in real life it is different. Most men and women are forced to perform parts for which they have no qualifications.

The world is a stage, but the play is badly cast.

Lord Savile's Crime

Life cheats us with shadows, like a puppet-master. We ask it for pleasure. It gives it to us, with bitterness and disappointment in its train.

For when one looks back upon the life that was so vivid in its emotional intensity, and filled with such fervent moments of ecstasy or joy, it all seems to be a dream and an illusion.

The Critic as Artist

The secret of life is to appreciate the pleasure of being terribly, terribly deceived.

The secret of life is to resist temptation.

A Woman of No Importance

Listening

It is a very dangerous thing to listen. If one listens one may be convinced; and a man who allows himself to be convinced by an argument is a thoroughly unreasonable person.

An Ideal Husband

One should never listen. To listen is a sign of indifference to one's hearers.

A Few Maxims for the Instruction of the Over-Educated

Literature

Literature always anticipates life. It does not copy it, but moulds it to its purpose.

The Decay of Lying

Love

Love is fed by the imagination, by which we become wiser than we know, better than we feel, nobler than we are: by which we can see Life as a whole; by which and by which alone, we can understand others in their real as in their ideal relations.

Only what is fine, and finely conceived, can feed Love.

Love can read the writing on the remotest star.

Love does not traffic in a marketplace, nor use a huckster's scales. Its joy, like the joy of the intellect, is to feel itself alive.

The aim of Love is to love: no more and no less.

There is no prison in any world into which Love cannot force an entrance.

De Profundis

Only love can keep anyone alive.

Who, being loved, is poor?

All love is terrible. All love is tragedy.

A Woman of No Importance

All lives, save loveless lives, true Love should pardon. A man's love is like that. It is wider, larger, more human than a woman's.

All I do know is that life cannot be understood without much charity, cannot be lived without much charity. It is love, and not German philosophy, that is the true explanation of this world, whatever may be the explanation of the next.

An Ideal Husband

Lying

Lying and poetry are arts – and they require the most careful study, the most disinterested devotion.

Lord Savile's Crime

Marriage

One can always know at once whether a man has home claims upon his life or not. I have noticed a very, very sad expression in the eyes of so many married men.

More marriages are ruined nowadays by the common sense of the husband than by anything else. How can a woman be expected to be happy with a man who insists on treating her as if she was a perfectly rational being?

Marriage is a sacrament for those who love each other.

A Woman of No Importance

You don't seem to realize, that in married life three is
company and two is none.

The Importance of Being Earnest

Loveless marriages are horrible. But there is one thing
worse than an absolutely loveless marriage. A marriage in
which there is love, but on one side only; faith, but on one
side only; devotion but on one side only, and in which of
the two hearts one is sure to be broken.

An Ideal Husband

Masks

Man is least himself when he talks in his own person. Give
him a mask, and he will tell you the truth.

The Critic as Artist

Men

We have all feet of clay, women as well as men; but when
we men love women, we love them knowing their
weaknesses, their follies, their imperfections, love them all
the more, it may be for that reason. It is not the perfect,
but the imperfect who have need of love.

An Ideal Husband

I have always been of the opinion that a man who desires
to get married should know either everything or nothing.

The General was essentially a man of peace, except in his
domestic life.

The Importance of Being Earnest

When a man is old enough to do wrong he should be old
enough to do right also.

A Woman of No Importance

Every great man nowadays has his disciples, and it is always
Judas who writes the biography.

The Critic As Artist

Misanthropy

A misanthrope I can understand – a womanthrope, never!

The Importance of Being Earnest

Modern painters

Most of our modern painters are doomed to absolute
oblivion. They never paint what they see. They paint
what the public sees, and the public never sees anything.

The Decay of Lying

Optimism

Optimism begins in a broad grin, and Pessimism ends with
blue spectacles. Besides, they are both of them merely
poses.

An Ideal Husband

Pain

Pain, unlike Pleasure, wears no mask.

De Profundis

Past

What lies before me is my past. I have got to make myself
look on that with different eyes, to make God look on it
with different eyes. This I cannot do by ignoring it, or
slighting it, or praising it or denying it. It is only to be
done by fully accepting it as an inevitable part of the
evolution of my life and character: by bowing my head to
everything I have suffered.

De Produndis

No one should be entirely judged by their past.

One's past is what one is. It is the only way by which
people should be judged.

An Ideal Husband

People

I always like the last person who is introduced to me; but as a rule, as soon as I know people I get tired of them.

Lord Savile's Crime

Politics

I adore political parties. They are the only places left to us where people don't talk politics.

An Ideal Husband

Principles

Circumstances should never alter principles!

An Ideal Husband

Public opinion

England has done one thing; it has invented and established Public Opinion, which is an attempt to organize the ignorance of the community, and to elevate it to the dignity of physical force.

The Critic as Artist

Public opinion exists only where there are no ideas.

A Few Maxims for the Instruction of the Over-Educated

Punishment

The gods are strange. It is not of our vices only they make instruments to scourge us. They bring us to ruin through what in us is good, gentle, humane, loving.

De Profundis

Question

It is always worth while asking a question, though it is not always worth while answering one.

An Ideal Husband

Romance

Romance should never begin with sentiment. It should
begin with science and end with a settlement.

An Ideal Husband

Twenty years of romance! Is there such a thing?

A Woman of No Importance

Shakespeare

Shakespeare might have met Rosencrantz and Guildenstern
in the white streets of London, or seen the rival houses
bite their thumbs at each other in the open square; but
Hamlet came out of his soul, and Romeo out of his
passion.

Sin

What is termed Sin is an essential element of progress.
Without it the world would stagnate, or grow old, or
become colourless. By its curiosity, Sin increases the
experience of the race.

The Critic as Artist

Sincerity

A little sincerity is a dangerous thing, and a great deal of it
is absolutely fatal.

The Critic as Artist

Society

In modern life nothing produces such an effect as a good
platitude. It makes the whole world kin.

An Ideal Husband

Oh! it is absurd to have a hard-and-fast rule about what
one should read and what one shouldn't. More than half
of modern culture depends on what one shouldn't read.

It is very vulgar to talk about one's business. Only people like stockbrokers do that, and then merely at dinner parties.

The Importance of Being Earnest

Society is a necessary thing. No man has any real success in this world unless he has got women to back him, and women rule society. If you have not got women on your side you are quite over.

A Woman of No Importance

We call ourselves a utilitarian age, and we do not know the uses of any single thing. We have forgotten that Water can cleanse, and Fire purify, and that the Earth is mother to us all.

De Profundis

Sorrow

There is nothing that stirs in the whole world of thought or motion to which sorrow does not vibrate in terrible if exquisite pulsation...It is a wound that bleeds when any hand but that of Love touches it and even then must bleed again, though not for pain.

To those who are in prison, tears are a part of every day's experience. A day in prison on which one does not weep is a day on which one's heart is hard, not a day on which one's heart is happy.

De Profundis

Hearts live by being wounded. Pleasure may turn a heart to stone, riches may make it callous, but sorrow – oh sorrow, cannot break it.

A Woman of No Importance

Stupidity

People cry out against the sinner, yet it is not the sinful, but the stupid who are our shame. There is no sin except stupidity.

The Critic as Artist

Style

In matters of grave importance, style, not sincerity is the vital thing.

The Importance of Being Earnest

Thought

It is so easy for people to have sympathy with suffering. It is so difficult for them to have sympathy with thought.

The Critic as Artist

Triviality

The trivial in thought and action is charming. I had made it the keystone of a very brilliant philosophy expressed in plays and paradoxes.

De Profundis

Truth

Truth, indeed, is a thing that is most painful to listen to and most painful to utter.

De Profundis

For what is truth? In matters of religion, it is simply the opinion that has survived. In matters of science, it is the ultimate sensation. In matters of art, it is one's last mood.

The Critic as Artist

War

As long as war is regarded as wicked, it will always have its
fascination. When it is looked upon as vulgar, it will cease
to be popular.

The Critic as Artist

Wealth

What this century worships is wealth. The God of this
century is wealth. To succeed one must have wealth. At all
costs one must have wealth.

An Ideal Husband

Weather

Whenever people talk to me about the weather, I always
feel quite certain that they mean something else. And that
makes me so nervous.

The Importance of Being Earnest

Wine

To know the vintage and quality of a wine one need not
drink the whole cask.

The Critic as Artist

Women

Ah! the strength of women comes from the fact that
psychology cannot explain us. Men can be analysed,
women ... merely adored.

One should never give a woman anything that she can't
wear in the evening.

There is only one real tragedy in a woman's life. The fact
that her past is always her lover, and her future invariably
her husband.

An Ideal Husband

English women conceal their feelings till after they are married. They show them then.

Plain women are always jealous of their husbands, beautiful women never are!

Every woman is a rebel, and usually in wild revolt against herself.

Women are hard on each other.

A Woman of No Importance

Work

It is awfully hard work doing nothing. However, I don't mind hard work where there is no definite object of any kind.

The Importance of Being Earnest

Youth

There is nothing like youth. The middle-aged are mortgaged to Life. The old are in life's lumber room. But youth is the Lord of Life.

All homage is delightful to an artist, and doubly sweet when youth brings it. Laurel and bay leaf wither when aged hands pluck them.

De Profundis

Bibliography

Oscar Wilde: A Biography (1976)
H Montgomery Hyde

Oscar Wilde (1987)
Richard Ellmann

The Portable Oscar Wilde
edited by
Richard Aldington and Stanley Weintaub (1946)

The Writings of Oscar Wilde
edited by
Isobel Murray (1989)